W9-BJZ-764

John Brown: The Making of a Martyr
Thirty-six Poems
Night Rider
Eleven Poems on the Same Theme
At Heaven's Gate
Selected Poems, 1923–1943
All the King's Men
Blackberry Winter
The Circus in the Attic
World Enough and Time
Brother to Dragons
Band of Angels
Segregation: The Inner Conflict in the South
Promises: Poems 1954–1956
Selected Essays
The Cave
All the King's Men (play)
You, Emperors, and Others: Poems 1957–1960
The Legacy of the Civil War
Wilderness
Flood
Who Speaks for the Negro?
Selected Poems: New and Old, 1923–1966
Incarnations: Poems 1966–1968
Audubon: A Vision
Homage to Theodore Dreiser
Meet Me in the Green Glen
Or Else—Poem/Poems 1968–1974
Democracy and Poetry
Selected Poems: 1923–1975
A Place to Come To
Now and Then: Poems 1976–1978
Brother to Dragons: A New Version
Being Here: Poetry 1977–1980
Jefferson Davis Gets His Citizenship Back
Rumor Verified: Poems 1979–1980
Chief Joseph of the Nez Perce

CHIEF
JOSEPH
of the
NEZ
PERCE

R A N D O M

H O U S E

N E W   Y O R K

CHIEF JOSEPH

of the

NEZ PERCE

Who Called Themselves

the Nimipu

"The Real People"

A POEM BY

ROBERT PENN WARREN

An earlier version of this poem appeared in
The Georgia Review.

Library of Congress Cataloging in Publication Data
Warren, Robert Penn, 1905–
Chief Joseph of the Nez Perce, who called themselves
the Nimipu—"the real people."
"An earlier version of this poem appeared in
The Georgia Review"—T.p. verso.
1. Joseph, Nez Percé Chief, 1840–1904—Poetry.
2. Nez Percé Indians—Poetry.
3. Indians of North America—Poetry.
I. Title.
PS3545.A748C5   1983   811'.52   82–20431
ISBN 0–394–53019–5
ISBN 0–394–71356–7 (pbk.)
ISBN 0–394–53038–1 (lim. ed.)

Manufactured in the United States of America
98765432
First Edition
Book design: Elissa Ichiyasu

"Made by the same Great Spirit, and living in the same land with our brothers, the red men, we consider ourselves as the same family; we wish to live with them as one people, and to cherish their interests as our own."

THOMAS JEFFERSON: TO THE MIAMIS, POWTEWATAMINIES, AND WEEAUKI

"The more we can kill this year, the less will have to be killed the next war, for the more I see of these Indians, the more convinced I am that they will all have to be killed or be maintained as a species of paupers."

WILLIAM TECUMSEH SHERMAN

"When the last Red Man shall have perished, and the memory of my tribe shall have become a myth among the white men, these shores will swarm with the invisible dead of my tribe, and when your children's children think themselves alone in the field, the store, the shop, upon the highway, or in the silence of the pathless woods, they will not be alone . . . At night when the streets of your cities are silent and you think them deserted, they will throng with the returning hosts that one filled them and still love this beautiful land. The White Man will never be alone."

CHIEF SEALTH OF THE DUWAMISH

Note

The Nez Percé (modernly Nez Perce) entered history as the friendly hosts to the explorers Lewis and Clark, and took care of their superfluous possessions when the expedition made the last push to the Pacific. The Nez Perce were a handsome and very vigorous people, but not basically warlike; and in general they refused scalping. They moved about with the offerings of the seasons, digging camas root, taking salmon at the time of their run, and making long hunts, across the Bitterroot Mountains into what is now Montana, for buffalo, which had already disappeared from their land by the time of Lewis and Clark. The Nez Perce, however, were not nomadic in the sense of the Plains Indians and were, for the most part, devoted to their homelands—for old Joseph and his famous son, this being Wallowa, in northeastern Oregon. The lands where the fathers were buried were sacred, and, in their version of immortality, the fathers kept watch on sons to be sure that truth was spoken, and that each showed himself a man.

The first treaty, of 1855, guaranteed the homeland of each band of the Nez Perce (for the Nez Perce were divided into "bands," each with its own organization, and each band being a signatory to the treaty). But after the gold rush of 1860, and the seizure of the guaranteed grants of bands in Idaho, the Federal Government proposed, in 1863, a treaty by which a restricted reservation, centered at Lapwai in Idaho, would include all the Nez Perce. Certain Indians in Idaho, already Christianized to a degree, accepted and signed. But other bands, including that of Joseph, stood on the treaty of 1855 and refused to sign, and remained on their homelands. In 1873, President Grant again guaranteed, in his own hand, Wallowa to Joseph's band, but, under pressure, then turned to the doomed experiment of trying to divide the region between Indians and whites.

In the end, Joseph's band (the young Joseph now being chief) was ordered to the reservation, in the worst season of the year and with little time. They painfully set out to obey overwhelming force, but after an outbreak of violence, in which they had no hand, they were attacked by Federal troops. The troops were routed with heavy loss, but the war had begun with a shot fired on the white flag of the Indians. This occurred on June 17, 1877.

On September 5, 1877, Joseph surrendered to Colonel Miles, in eastern Montana. The terms given by Miles were generous, but these were murderously broken by Sherman, now Commanding General of the U.S. Army. Chief Joseph's life now became a constant struggle for the observation of the terms of Miles, but only after many years and many deaths were his people returned to the high country of the Northwest—though not to Wallowa.

Joseph and 150 Nez Perce were confined on a reservation in northeastern Washington. It seems that Joseph never gave up hope of returning to Wallowa, but in vain. On September 21, 1904, in the exile at Colville, Washington, sitting before his fire, he fell dead. The physician of Colville, somewhat unscientifically, filed the report that the chief had died of a broken heart.

CHIEF
JOSEPH
of the
NEZ
PERCE

I

The Land of the Winding Waters, Wallowa,
The Land of the Nimipu,
Land sacred to the band of old Joseph,
Their land, the land in the far ages given
By the Chief-in-the-Sky. Their ponies, crossed
With the strong blood of horses, well-bred, graze
Richly the green blade. Boys, bareback, ride naked,
Leap on, shout "Ai-yah!" Shout "Ai-yee!"—
In unbridled glory. Eagle wing catches sun.
Gleams white. Boys plunge into water, gay as
The otter at gambol, with flat hands slap water
Like beaver tails slapping to warn, then dive,
Beaverlike, to depth, toes leaving the shimmer,
Uncoiling upward, of bubbles. On sandbars
Boys stretch, they yawn, and sun dries the skin
To glints gold, red, bronze. Each year
They go where from seaward salmon, infatuate,
Unfailing at falls-leap, leap great stones. They leap
The foaming rigor of current—seeking, seeking,
In blind compulsion, like fate, the spawn-
Pool that blood remembers. What does our blood,
In arteries deep, heaving with pulse-thrust
In its eternal midnight, remember?
We stir in sleep. We, too, belong
To the world, and it is spread for our eyes.

*

The salmon leaps, and is the Sky-Chief's blessing.
The Sky-Power thus blessed the Nimipu
And blessed them, too, with
The camas root, good to the tongue, in abundance.

> *Their honesty is immaculate and their purity of purpose*
> *and their observance of the rules of their religion are most*
> *uniform and remarkable. They are certainly more like a*
> *nation of saints than a horde of savages.*

JEAN BAPTISTE LE MOYNE DE BIENVILLE

It is their land, and the bones of their fathers
Yet love them, and in that darkness, lynxlike,
See how their sons still thrive without fear,
Not lying, not speaking with forkèd tongue.
Men know, in night-darkness, what wisdom thrives with the fathers.

By campfire at night old chiefs tell young boys
How first the "crowned ones," white men with head covered,
Had come, and their great war-chief, with honor,
Clean hands and medals and gifts, had sat
On the blanket with chiefs, and Chief Twisted-Hair
Had drawn on white elk-hide the way west,
Where boomed the Great Water Ill-Tasted—at land's end,
Where storms, winter long, strode those waters, with might.

The white chief went. Returning, said, yes.

"I was born at the time of snow. My name—
 It was Miats Ta-weet Tu-eka-kas,
 The son of my father Tu-eka-kas.
 But not my true name. Only after ten snows
 Was I, a boy, ready to climb
 Alone to the mountain, to lie with no motion
 On the stone-bed I made, no food, no water, heart open
 To vision. To float as in vision and see
 At last, at last, my Guardian Spirit
 Come to protect me and give forth my true name.
 Three days I lay on the mountain, heart open.
 All day stared into bright blue. All night
 Into darkening air. Then vision, it came.
 But by day, clear. An old man, he stood
 And he gave me a name. I learned to say it.

"I went down the mountain. My father I could not
 Yet tell. But when the new-named ones, they danced,
 Each dancing his new name, I danced. I leaped,
 Skyward pointing, exclaiming, *Hin-mah-toó-yah-lat-kekht*—
 Thunder-Traveling-to-Loftier-Mountain-Heights. That
 Was my name. That made my medicine true.

*

5

"My father—Old Joseph, whites called him—had heard
Of the 'New Book of Heaven' the whites had brought
To Lapwai—the Place of the Butterflies—
And how it gave the heart brightness. So went there.
Lapwai was then not named reservation
As later it was for those who sold
Their land to the white man. But no!—
For us never—who sold not the sacred
Bones of our fathers for white-man money,
And food-scraps.

"But far in Lapwai, my father
Longed for the sacred Winding Waters,
And came there, yet carried the 'New Book of Heaven,'
New in our tongue now. But could he forget
The bones of his fathers, and the Old Wisdom?
Nor eyes of the fathers that watch from darkness?

"So was not at Lapwai, when firewater came. And the killing.

"Again 'crowned heads,' they came, the makers of treaties.
They sought out my father in friendship, with paper and ink."

> *For the South Nez Perces; commencing where the*
> *southern tributary of the Palouse River flows from spurs*
> *of Bitter Root Mountains; thence down said tributary to*
> *the mouth of Ti-nat-pan-up Creek, thence southerly to the*
> *crossing of the Snake ten miles below the mouth of the*
> *Alpowa River; thence to the source of Alpowa River in*
> *the Blue Mountains; thence to the crossing of Grande*

Rond River, midway along the divide between the waters
Wol-low-how and Powder Rivers; thence to the crossing of
the Snake River fifteen miles below mouth of Powder
River; thence Salmon River fifty miles above crossing;
then along spurs of Bitter Root Mountains to the place of
beginning.

NEZ PERCES CESSION, 1855

"I, a boy, stood and watched my father.
His hand reached out. It made the name-mark.
And why not? Not once had we shed white blood
Since the first great war-chief on the blanket had sat
With Twisted-Hair, and had named the land ours.
Now in ink was promised the Winding Waters forever,
Where sacred bones lay, and we knew them sacred.
We were promised also our land fit for snow-time,
For we knew the sacred wheel of the seasons.

"A promise, how pretty!—but our sacred land
They trod. They spat on our earth. It was like
A man's spit on your face. I, then a boy,
I felt the spit on my face. New treaties
They drew up to bind us with thongs. But only
The false Nimipu signed, those who already
Had gone to Lapwai, which was now reservation—
To eat, like a beggar, stale bread of white men.
Yes, they—only they—would sign. No! No!
Not ever my father. Never. Nor I."

"How far away, and wavering
  Like mist in dawn wind, was the law! You have seen
  How mist in creek bottoms to nothing burns
  When the sun-blaze strikes. How far away
  Sat the Great White Father!
  But we heard how in his heart he holds goodness.
  His word came to us to give rejoicing."

"But it faded like mist in the day's heat."

II

"But what is a piece of white paper, ink on it?
What if the Father, though great, be fed
On lies only, and seeks not to know what
Truth is, or cannot tell Truth from Lie?
So tears up the paper of Truth, and the liars,
Behind their hands, grin, while he writes a big Lie?

"Yes, what is a piece of white paper with black
Marks? And what is a face, white,
With lips tight shut to hide forkèd tongue?
Too late, too late, we knew what was the white spot
In distance—white cover of cloth, leather-tough,
On wagons that gleamed, like white clouds adrift
Afar, far off, over ridges in sunlight:
But they knew where they went, and we knew.
This knowledge, like lead of a rifle, sagged heavy in flesh—
Healed over, but there. It ached in the night."

> *But no recollection of former services could stand*
> *before the white man's greed.*
>
> MAJOR J. C. TRIMBLE

"My father held my hand, and he died.
Dying, said: 'Think always of your country.

Your father has never sold your country.
Has never touched white-man money that they
Should say they have bought the land you now stand on.
You must never sell the bones of your fathers—
For selling that, you sell your Heart-Being.' "

*I think it a great mistake to take from Joseph and his band
of Nez Perces Indians that valley [Wallowa].*

GENERAL O. O. HOWARD

"Into a dark place my father had gone.
You know how the hunter, at dawn, waits,
String notched, where the buck comes to drink. Waits,
While first light brightens highest spruce bough, eyes slitted
Like knife wounds, breath with no motion. My father
Waits thus in his dark place. Waiting, sees all.
Sees the green worm on green leaf stir. Sees
The aspen leaf turn though no wind, sees
The shadow of thought in my heart—the lie
The heel must crush. Before action, sees
The deed of my hand. My hope is his Wisdom.

"Oh, open, Great Spirit, my ears, my heart,
To his sky-cry as though from a snow-peak of distance!"

*It cannot be expected that Indians . . . will . . . submit
without any equivalent to be deprived of their homes and
possessions or to be driven off to some other locality where
they cannot find their usual means of subsistence . . . It*

"Does a grain of gold, in the dark ground, lie
Like a seed-sprout? What color of bloom
Will it bear? What cunning has it to make
Men rive raw rock where it hides like a murderous secret?
What cunning to lie in innocent brightness
Like wet sand in water? In water, what dives
The deepest—deep, deeper than the lead pellet?

"For all things live, and live in their nature.
But what is the nature of gold?

"In the deepest dark what vision may find it?
On its stone-bed of vision what secret name be divulged?
If it could dance in the name-dance, what
Name would gold dance? Would it be—
Death-that-in-darkness-comes-smiling?

"Or is it man's nature this thing not to know?"

"Years fled. But with heart grown small, as from fear,
   What man can live forever? True,
   We had long back made the promise of peace.
   We had sworn no white blood to shed, our tongue was not forkèd.
   But now we breathed the stink of the wind of Time,
   As when wind comes bad from the death of the promise of peace—
   As when on the big plain from upwind taint comes
   From the age-dead old buffalo cow that rots in the sun.
   You wake at night, not believing the dream's stink.
   You try to think: 'I lie here as always,
   In my own tepee, at peace with all men.'

"But think of your father's eyes in his darkness.

"The sun rises up. No end to the dream's stink."

> *I call him* [the Indian] *a savage, and I call a savage
> something wholly desirable to be civilized off the face of the
> earth.*
>
> CHARLES DICKENS

"You stand in the sun. You think: 'Am I Joseph?'
   You find yourself watching the white man's horse-soldiers,
   How they ride two-by-two, four-by-four, how they swing
   Into line, charge or stop, dismount.
   How the holders of horses fall back, while others
   Are forming for skirmish. Or deploying for cover.

"The white horse-soldiers, they mount from the left.
   We from right. Can that be a difference?

*

"Still as a stone, I stand watching, then suddenly know
   How the young men watch me. Tears come to my eyes,
   For I think how bodies, dead, in moonlight would shine.
   I watch how the horse-soldiers wheel into line.
   The young men watch me. One finger I touch
   To my brow. Trace lines there. Then lay
   A hand to my breast. It is hard to stand
   And not know what self you have lived with, all years.
   Oh, how can such two Truths kiss in your heart?

"For now you know what a treaty is—
   Black marks on white paper, black smoke in the air.
   For the greatest white war-chief—they call him Chief One-Arm—
   Chief Howard—now in a loud voice he calls.
   At a council of those who would take us away
   From our land forever, at last I stood.

"In my weakness, tongue dry to the arch of my mouth,
   I stood. My people waited. They waited
   For words, for wisdom, to pass my lips—
   Lips more dry than dust. Before me, I saw
   All the blue coats, the buttons of gold, the black
   Coats buttoned up tight
   Over bellies that bulged—
   White and sweaty, you knew, under that cloth—
   And softer than dough. My words
   Could not come. I saw
   Their lips curl. I saw them,
   Behind hands held up, in secret sneer.
   'Oh, who will speak!' cried the heart in my bosom.
   'Speak for the Nimipu, and speak Truth!'

*

"But then, my heart, it heard
  My father's voice, like a great sky-cry
  From snow-peaks in sunlight, and my voice
  Was saying the Truth that no
  White man can know, how the Great Spirit
  Had made the earth but had drawn no lines
  Of separation upon it, and all
  Must remain as He made, for to each man
  Earth is the Mother and Nurse, and to that spot
  Where he was nursed, he must,
  In love cling."

> *The earth, my mother and nurse, is very sacred to me: too
> sacred to be valued, or sold for gold or for silver . . . and my
> bands have suffered wrong rather than done wrong.*
>
> CHIEF JOSEPH TO THE COMMISSIONERS OF 1876

"Howard understood not. He showed us the rifle.
  The rifle is not what is spoken in peace-talk.
  He says we must leave the Winding Waters
  Forever, forever—
  Or come the horse-soldiers.
  We must live afar with a shrunk-little heart,
  And dig in the ground like a digger of roots—at Lapwai,
  The Place of the Butterflies—how pretty
  That name for a reservation to puke on!
  Far from the fatherly eyes that stare in darkness.
  Far from my father's words—and my promise!
  So my chin to my chest dug deep. For I knew

One-Arm's numbers, and all those behind him.
I knew the strange gun that spits bullets like hail.
It sits on its wheels and spits bullets like hail.

"Worse—thirty days only to leave Wallowa,
  With horses and herds, our old, young, and sick.
  Horses and herds, they swam, though the Snake,
  In thaw-flood, snatched off the weak colts, the weak calves,
  And whites stole the rest left with poor guard.
  But in round boats of buffalo hide, the people
  Already were over, four strong horses and riders
  To swim with each boat, and push for the shore.

"Even so, our young braves, they swallowed their rage,
  Like bile that burns in the belly, and waits.
  No, not ours it was who brought the great grief,
  But young men of Chief White Bird.
  They fled, burned houses, soaked earth with blood."

III

"But on *our* trail, horse-soldiers in darkness came,
  With hope to surprise us. Fools—
  With gear jangle and horse fart! Though we needed not that.
  At the heart of the night we heard what we heard—
  The wailful howl of the sad coyote.
  But no coyote! It was our scout.
  He lay there in darkness, owl-eyed, deer-eared.
  At dawn they came to surprise us.
  Surprise!—It was theirs.

"We, who wanted no blood-spill, we sent a white flag.
  But we knew not their heart, so young braves
  Were stripping for battle. Ponies
  Tossed head. Though many braves snored yet. Snored
  From firewater the killers had stolen, then sneaked in
  For refuge. Like hogs they snored. Vomit flecked lips.

"So what had we? Of braves, had only
  Some threescore, and poor-armed, old trade guns
  You load at death-lip, old shotguns, or Winchesters
  Fewer than ten. Then bows—but bows
  With love worked from the horn of wild sheep,
  And backed with sheep tendon, and I have seen,
  In the thundering chase, a young hunter set
  His *flèche* feather-deep to probe the heart

Of the running buffalo bull, and the bull
Stumbles. Our young men, like shadows,
Were gone now, some left, some right, to cover
The draw's depth. To wait peace or war.

"The horse-soldiers stood. The white flag approached,
With the heart's true invitation. But what peace
Can there be when a shot is the only answer?
A man in a white hat, no soldier, fired it.
But how could we know? So soldiers died. From every draw,
Ledge, sage clump, death peered, death came.
Thirsty the sands of the canyon—oh, thirsty!
Death came with the whispering slyness of arrows.
Came with the whistling nag of hot lead.
On a prong-stick you prop your barrel, aim steady.
Not *bang-bang* like soldiers. You husband your powder.

"Then bursts the charge of the braves on their ponies—
The war-whoop, the *whang* of arrows at short-range.
The last of the battle formation is shattered
Like the buffalo herd stampeded at cliff-edge.
The sands redder go. Like old women, some soldiers
Lose mounts. Flee on foot.
In blind corners die.
All flee. Miles we chase them. Coats, weapons, we take.
Scalps never. We touch not the locks of the honored dead.
Now rifles we have, sixty-three by our count.
Now braves hide their bows. Now rifles they have!
And pistols. Ah, the white friend is kind!"

"Yes, rifles we had now. But braves so few.
  And white men, they swirl down like snowflakes in winter.
  Hope we had of the great Looking Glass,
  A war-chief with paw of cougar, and cunning
  Of fox. We sent word. For he was our blood.
  But no, but no, he dreamed he might live
  In peace. But soon knew it only
  A dream. To his village, horse-soldiers—they came.
  They called for surrender. But Looking Glass answered
  He was not at war. So a white man fired.
  Killed only a baby.

"So Looking Glass, the wise, the brave,
  Came to sit in our council of chiefs, the great war-chief!
  White fools, they gave him to us, like a present.

"Chief Howard, Great One-Arm—his hundreds now come,
  With big-bellied belch-gun and those that spit pellets.
  Across the Salmon, yet flooding, we teased them, we lured them."

"Across the flood-Salmon, like children they came
 With all their fool tangle of cables and ferries,
 Into our mountains, the trails mud-slick,
 Roped pack-mules plunging down cliffside, the forest
 In darkness at sun-height. Then we, easy,
 Cross over the river. Cross back. On the plain are free
 To meet soldiers, scout parties. We meet, and they die.
 And in the dark mountains the War-Chief-Who-Prays
 Now prayed for supplies. Cut off for three days,
 With bellies growling, guts flat, he at last
 Made the river with all that aimless tackle and gear.

"At Clearwater, then, we fought them. We held.
 For two days we held them, locked in our circle,
 While old, young, sick, and women, by travois escaped.
 But, oh, not back to the Winding Waters!"

The Indians fought like devils and were brave as lions.

CAPTAIN BANCROFT
(WOUNDED, FROM HOSPITAL AT LAPWAI)

"We tried to be brave like men, we tried
 To cleanse hearts.
 To make acceptable medicine.
 But the Great Spirit turned his face away
 From the land of the Winding Waters we loved.

"Did he turn his face because of my heart-pride?
 Because I was proud to sit in the council

With war-chiefs, the great ones, adept at blood skills?
They knew cunning deceits but never knew soul-fear.
I was proud to sit there, and always my ears
Pricked forward for wisdom, as the wolf pricks ears
At a rustle on soft wind,
For I stored all I heard for the heart's lonely thought,
To be ready, be strong, when the moment came.
Sometimes in battle I took care of those
Too old, too young, or too sick. To give them
Their safety. My Guardian Spirit, it told me.
But I, too, down the length of the death-tube have peered,
Squeezed trigger, seen blood spurt, have rallied
My braves. I knew the joy of the clamor.
I strove to be named by the name of a man.

"I have even devised a new death-trap and spoken
In council. And the first chief nodded. Then all."

> *The Great Spirit puts it into the heart and head of man to*
> *know how to defend himself.*
>
> CHIEF JOSEPH

"But later, ah, later, when men named that war
With my name, my heart in my bosom would tighten.
Would shrink. What praise does man want but his manhood?
We all had manhood, we showed at Clearwater."

> *I do not think that I had to exercise more thorough*
> *generalship during the Civil War than I did in the march*

GENERAL O. O. HOWARD

"But what was the good of our sweated blood?—
Howard behind us, the mountain wall eastward.
From Howard no peace terms, and eastward only
Lolo Pass, which crawled up in cloud-heights,
And we knew that Howard would try to cut Lolo.
For me, I would stand, fight, and die, if only
In dream of my sacred land, but the chiefs
In council said *no*. Looking Glass said *no*.
And I heeded their wisdom. What right had I
To die—to leave sick, old, young, women—merely to flatter
My heart's pride? For a true chief no self has. So up,
Up Lolo, track ragged and rocky, crag-dark,
Belabored by deadfall, but with hope
To find at the end of long travail Sitting Bull,
Who now sat safe by the 'skirts of the Old Lady Queen,'
Far northward. He would know us as men.

"Howard, we raced him. Won. But eastward
New soldiers had a fort built to trap us. Now under
White flag we held pow-wow for peace. Meanwhile,
Our scouts smelled a way. Hard and bitter it was.
But the east goes red with dawn—and ho!—
Here only some last coals now dying, all night,
Kept alive for deceit. We had flung out a screen

Of braves behind ledges, rim-rock, tree-growth,
So they dared not leave that fort ill-placed.
Some tried, but not living to hear the gray hornet's song
Before its kiss came.

" 'Fort Fizzle,' they called it. Fort Fizzle it was.
　But yet no way to get to the 'Old Lady's Skirts.'

　"So up Bitterroot, friendly with settlements,
　Trading with farmers, for guns, ammunition,
　Not killing, laughing together. Then eastward,
　Toward grass of the buffalo land, and high sky.
　Peace-thinking deceived us. We thought we were free."

I V

"Near dawn they struck us, new horse-soldiers. Shot
Into tepees. Women, children, old died.
Some mothers might stand in the river's cold coil
And hold up the infant and weep, and cry mercy.
What heart beneath blue coat has fruited in mercy?
When the slug plugged her bosom, unfooting her
To the current's swirl and last darkness, what last
Did she hear? It was laughter.

"And we, we were blind, blind in the bushes,
Rage-blind, hearts burning, hides naked except for
Snatched bandoliers, rifles foolish in hand—but then!
Then the great voice of Looking Glass, White Bird's war-whoop,
Its terrible quaver! We heard, turned,
Saw horse-soldiers laughing, bright milling in firelight.
And, sudden, we knew our darkness a blessing. Few there
Laughed long. Light summoned hot lead from darkness.
Few managed to flee to high cover. Dug holes
In the ground. But our rifles found any that stirred.
And dawn filled the canyon.

"We took their big-bellied gun that belched. We broke it.
New rifles we had, new boots, new coats—
From bodies, white humps gleaming in sunshine,
And now clutching earth as though they had loved her.

*

"Few laughed as naked they lay there. Our own hearts
  Were swollen with rage, but rage like great joy.
  And gratefulness. The Chief-in-the-Sky—
  He had seen our need. He smiled on us.
  He said: 'Know now you are men. Be men!'

"With his help we were men. And scouts out now always."

> *I could smell white people, the soldiers, a long way . . .*
> *My Guardian Spirit instructed that I scout mostly alone.*
> *None of the enemies had appeared coming on our last sun's*
> *trail . . . I watched if antelope acted curious. It might be*
> *danger. If prairie birds flew up in distance, it might be*
> *buffalo stampeding . . . The unexpected shadow against*
> *a big rock.*
>
> YELLOW WOLF, SCOUT OF THE NEZ PERCE

"Yes, never again did the sunrise come
  Without, at first light, a far shadow on ridge-spine
  To wheel, wave blanket, ho! At night had that scout
  Snaked nearer and nearer a campfire? The sleeper
  Breathed steady. A throat might be slit, and the sleeper
  With no breath to moan. For a hand blocked the mouth.
  And scouts at distance knew how to direct
  The far anger of Enfield, or Spencer, or Sharps.
  Men have fallen from saddle before echo came.
  Men have fallen face-down in a skillet when cooking.

"All night white men knew eyes to be watching.
  *

"All night scouts wore wolf-skins. In darkness wolves called.

"Past lava, past schist, past desert and sand—
A strange land we wandered to eastern horizons
Where blueness of mountains swam in their blue—
In blue beyond name. The hawk hung high.
Gleamed white. A sign. It gleamed like a word in the sky.
Cleanse hearts and pray. Pray to know what the Sky-Chief
Would now lean to tell. To the pure heart, Truth speaks.

"We dreamed to enter the pass they name Tachee,
The land where Evil Spirits may dwell,
Where water may stink, and a river stink evil,
And the ulcerous earth boils foul.
But we trusted the will of the Sky-Chief to lead us,
To lead us the way of silence and shadow.
We dreamed of the mountain where one drop of dew
At noon yet hangs at the pine-needle tip
And speaks back to no sun. We dreamed.
But no. Not yet.

"To your belly the plant of the camas is kind.
Women gather the root on the camas prairies.
It is a gift from our Great Earth Mother—
But only for us. The white man spits on it,
Blaspheming. And to the white man it gave back,
At last, one word. And Death was the word.
On Camas Meadows we found him. In moon-dark,
In columns of two, as though soldier-saddles we rode.
We sat up as soldiers, as though the friendly
Patrol returning. We knew a patrol out.

*

"We rode in close. Challenge, at last!
  Then war-whoop, the blaze,
  Tent canvas tattered by bullets, the death-scream, the mule train
  Stampeding after the bell of the lead-mare
  Now rung by a brave who had crept in to steal it
  And now dashed onward, and on,
  Into darkness and distance. Thus
  It began. Some ran from their weapons."

> NARRATION: *Some were crying. They ran, and one voice*
> *called loudly for them to come back to their guns.*
> QUERY: *Where were the guns of the soldiers who were*
> *standing guard?*
> NARRATION: *The guns were stacked.*
> QUERY: *You did not really hear the soldiers crying, did you?*
> NARRATION: *I heard them cry like babies. They were bad*
> *scared.*
>
> INTERVIEW WITH INDIAN WARRIOR

"Then Tachee, the door to the friendship of mountains,
  And the world of the foot-soundless shadow. Ah, there!—
  There the mountains of Yellowstone, silence,
  The secret recesses. There the wolf-call
  Could be but a wolf in wolf-darkness, calling.
  You turn on your side. You sleep. Till dawn.

"What days, what nights, had we come in our harriment?
  Long, long the summer, but dawn-ice now blue.
  Remember your dead now lonely under

High stars with no name. Snow comes soon. In darkness, awake,
In new mountains, you stare up to see, bright as steel,
Stars wheel in unfamiliar formations. You know not
That sky. Nor that land, nor where foot leads.

"But there was one with us, of white and red blood
Together, but red was his heart, Poker Joe, and he knew
All the sly trails, deceits of the passes. In
That land of mountainous blankness, he scented in darkness,
He tasted the air. We trusted. He knew
The names of the mountains, in darkness
Their whisper he heard.

"And Howard's poor half-wits, with compass and maps,
Had traveled more than their thousand
Miles, steel of horseshoes thin-splitting, boot-leather
No longer saving the callus
From blood-scrape of razor-edge lava, or granite,
Coats threadbare for blasts from northward now fanged, the belly
Already growling in hunger's anxiety."

> *As it had been a severer tax upon the energies of officers*
> *and men than any period in the late Civil War, surely some*
> *method must be found to encourage and properly reward*
> *such gallantry and service hardly ever before excelled.*
>
> GENERAL O. O. HOWARD

"But we, our hearts leaned toward the mountains!
We could never starve in the Sky-Chief's goodness.

*

"Into that nightmare of chasm and peak,
We plunged. But no nightmare for Joe! How soft
The pine needles, padding the foot arch stone-strained,
Lava-cut! How gentle the silence as when
You wake, and the loving boughs lean! What if
Old One-Arm should come, as sure, in the end?
With new men, new supplies, new spit-guns, new boots?
And we guessed, before word of scouts, that eastward,
Where eye-into-eye mountains see sun come,
Already horse-soldiers were freshly counted
To grind us between a mortar and pestle."

V

Where east, and north, the mountain wall broke,
Stone fingers, with nails, stretched out at the plain,
And in between fingers were passes that westward
Became a gut-tangle of canyons, ravines, crevasses,
And cliff-sided slits no root could clutch, or bear claw,
And if you looked up, day was only a sky streak.
From high west to high east spine-ridges ran,
Peaks stabbing high beyond blackness
And clamber and shag of conifers. Who,
North or south, could make way that way? Yes,
Poker could, and Joseph, his people.

And Howard,
In blunder and bumble—yes, he was tough.
Would winch wagons—unwheeled front or rear—two hundred
Feet up, or worse. Then down. Then days
Later find he had cut
Across his own trail. Was sometimes, in fact,
As baffled as any idiot kitten that tangles
Itself in a ball of sock-wool, or a trot-line.

The only scouts Howard sent out not later found dead
Were those with news Poker wanted Howard to hear
As he staggered through the insane Absarokas—
That saber-jagged, murderous mania of mountains

And stream-yelping canyons where every
Direction is only a lie—hoping
At last to pin Joseph against Colonel Sturgis,
Who horse-held the plain, waiting, waiting—
For Sturgis, a son dead with Custer, was mad for revenge.

Yes, it would be
An operation brilliant in textbooks,
A nutcracker action—depending, of course,
On information and timing. But Howard,
His scouts all found dead or with useless news,
Hung ignorantly north
Near Clark Fork headwaters, waiting to strike.
But Sturgis, in hot haste and heat of revenge, was tricked
South, up the stinking Shoshone, and into the mountains,
Pursuing Joseph and Joe, with trail signs
All subtle but carefully clear,
To find, in the end, a well-trampled spot, a spot
Where ponies outward had circled and circled
To hide all trail thence—or generously give
Too God-damned many. But, ah, plainsward
Sturgis spies dust rise, the bands, of course!
Dust rose, swelling slow in the pale pink of dawn-shine.

So, "Halloo!" shouts Sturgis, hell-bent for the spooks.

For spooks, they were. Dust settles, and nothing
Is there but ripped pine boughs and sage clumps left
By braves now galloping north, and coiling their lariats—
Laughing.

*

Back now—back at the circle of trampled confusion
Devised by the wicked cunning of Joe or
The instinct of Joseph—or whose?—Sturgis found
The telltale spot where no dew seemed shaken from shyest leaf,
Where pebbles too perfectly showed no streak of mud.
And that, of course, was the route of escape, the magic
Of red men. It gave
On a knife-slice of canyon as dark as a tunnel,
And needle-narrow. It faded back north,
Reversing the track of Sturgis's drive for revenge.

Northward, it led, and Joseph could enter
The mystic path, past Howard, to
Clark's Fork and freedom.

V I

Now the last dash! The Great Spirit had smiled
On those who knew to endure or die,
And those who knew the joy of expending man's strength
That others might laugh in sunshine, and sing.

If you were the eyes of the Eagle of eagles,
And from vast height looked down on the bruised
Thumb-hump of the Little Bear Paw Mountains, then southward,
You'd see a tangle of canyon and coulee
Where water, long back, had sliced at the high plain;
And south then, plains of great grass curried
By wind-comb, or lying gray-green in its slickness
Of windless autumn sunlight, or worn down
By buffalo hoof or tooth-edge to earth's
Inner redness, and dust-devils rising in idle
Swirl, or the white-streaked poison of
Alkali flats, standing stakes of poplars long dead,
And farther, more canyons and coulees black
With shadow as sun saddens westward, and low.
Then, worn down by ages and ice-grind, the Little
Rockies, and, eastward crawling, the glitter
Of rivers, first the Missouri, then
Plains again, lounging and lazy, or plagued by dust-devils.
More mountains, the Moccasins reaching north-south,
The Judiths east-curving, and likewise the Big

Snowy Mountains, and farther some eighty miles,
Another glitter of river, slow, idle, eastward,
The Yellowstone, and from that level,
The bulge, hump, leap of the Great
Granite Peak, from which all earth falls away,
Past glacier, precipice, past rocks ripped
Like wounds from a grizzly's claws. —And there,
Two hundred miles off, slow, slow, in distance,
Almost invisible, even to Your eternal Eye, the advancing
Riffle of dust. They come.

Northward they move.
They move from the Land of the Evil Spirits unharmed.

But dimmer by distance, almost transparent
In late light, unformed as a thumb-smear, blue blur
On the sky's autumnal yellowness: Howard.

Old One-Arm, dogged, devout, knowing
Himself snared in God's cleft stick of justice,
Stirs in the saddle. His heart is military.
Is inflamed with love of glory and
Vanity wounded. He is the butt
Of every newspaper. Like foxfire,
At night in his dream, his quarry flickers, sardonic,
Before him. Does
He hear distant laughter in dream? By God,
Pursue! He will! The old wound
Aches. He thinks of Seven Pines. Well,
Let last leather split, feet bleed, last

Horseshoe be cast. Man
Is born to suffer. He is born to God's will.

But a stern chase, by land or sea,
Is a long chase. He knows that much.
His heart is iron. He has seen much blood. But
Against his will, his ambition, the heart
Melts in his breast. It
Suffers a flame of logic that
Vindictively flares through the straw
Of ambition, and he, in heart-pain, admits
That from Fort Keogh, northeast, Colonel Miles
Might, upward and west, strike a long angle
Of interception.

And receive surrender!

Nausea burns his throat. Acid of bile. What
Then for him, for Howard! For his
Long struggle, unflinching, over a thousand miles,
For anguish, defeats, his dead lying under
Unloving stars? His heart splits in prayer.
He has stood before his regiments on Sunday morning
To pray. Now, in darkness, he prays.

His heart splits,
Like a stone, red-hot, into snow cast.

He thinks of Miles. He thinks what all men know:
A groveling hem-kisser of the draggled skirts of glory.
He thinks of him. But,
Suddenly, with sad pity.

Orders, identical, go out. One by
Horse, one by boat. —And the heart of Miles at Keogh
Flares like a rocket. A general once—
But only of state militia. Now only
A colonel—regular, but rank reduced. His head goes dizzy
Like a drunkard's whose fingers close on the bottle.
In the infinite black firmament inside
His skull, a star, in explosion, blazes, bursts
In the birth of worlds. He knows now that
God loves him! Bugles blare.
Blare here! Blare there! Distance is nothing.

As Joseph drew northward, Howard drew on.
Joseph knew but one word: *north*. And northeast
The Yellowstone flowed, backed westward by yellow-
Gray rim-rock and shortening sunsets. Joseph,
His sick, his old, his young are now driven
Like wraiths in Joseph's iron dream.

*

Sturgis has his own blood-drenched dream.
His scouts feed his dream.
One more chance! He follows.
Oh, one more chance!

But Joseph drives on. He dreams
Of a break in the western bulwark of rim-rock
That backs the river—dreams
Of an opening, perhaps some creek coming in,
That looks wide and gracious, yet suddenly
Goes narrow, flanked by cliffs and crevasses,
Flange rock and rubble, a place where
One man is twenty—is fifty—if powder holds out. Oh,
For an opening wide, inviting, that,
Suddenly, like a lethal noose,
Tightens. He hacks at his scouts.

There—a gift of the Great Sky-Chief—
It is! And the sick, old, incompetent
Are huddled up-canyon. A few braves
Are set at the opening for bait and delay.

And Sturgis
Gave thanks to God, and struck!

The bait before him fades into the narrowing throttlement.
Poor Sturgis! He never could learn, and now crowded
His horsemen in until, at a burst, from
Flanges, shelves, rim-rocks, ledges, sage clumps,
The unhived lead hums happily honeyward.

*

Now Joseph long gone up the death-sweet canyon,
Howard arrived to survey the scene.
From saddle, he slowly surveyed it with more than
Professional eye:

> It was the most horrible of places—sage-brush and dirt,
> and only alkaline water, and very little of that! Dead horses
> were strewn around, and other relics of the battlefield! A
> few wounded and dead were there. To all this admixture of
> disagreeable things was added a cold, raw wind, that,
> unobstructed, swept over the country. Surely, if anything
> was needed to make us hate war such after-battle scenes
> come into play.

Yes, Joseph again gone—and Sturgis
Outfought in spite of men and equipment,
And pursuers unable to breach the inner bulwark of rim-rock!
Now, on the northern horizon, the dust
Of Joseph is lost. Southward, three armies,
In the saw-toothed Absarokas, had, breath-bated, lain
In wait, but Joseph's people, like water,
Like air, like ghosts, had slipped through the clutch of fingers.

But Joseph knew nothing of Miles, and his star.

Miles curses the cavalry, infantry, forward
To follow that flare in his head. In his saddle
Miles reels. The thought—it is ghastly! What if
Howard comes to find him merely holding Joseph at bay?
Then all—all—for naught. For Howard, outranking,

Would receive the surrender. Miles shuts eyes. Sees
In darkness the glare of newspaper headlines,
Far off, in New York. In Washington, too.
Then the merciless masonry of the news story.
Tears come to his eyes. He curses his laggards. And Howard.

On the western shore of the mountains, Joseph
Moves north four days, but slower, slower,
For Howard, in cunning, relaxes his pressure
That Miles, unknown, on the eastern slope
May drive on past, then strike a hook southward.

Joseph, at last, to the Little Bear Paws comes.
He believes himself safe by the "Old Lady's Skirts":

> *I sat down in a fat and beautiful country. I had won my
> freedom and the freedom of my people. There were many
> empty places in the lodges and the council, but we were in
> a land where we could not be forced to live in a place we
> did not want.*

Clearly defensible, in the alluvial gulch
Of Snake Creek, beside good water, they
Set themselves down, protected from wind
By bluffs, farther by mountains, tepees now set
In a circle, good hunting handy. Women
Could here dry winter meat, and livestock
Graze widely. But in precaution at each
Tepee a mount was staked. No scouts out, however.
For this was a land of peace. They had peace.

*

In dawn light this was the pastoral scene Miles saw—
And saw, or thought he saw, how the slope,
Wide, rolling, slightly atilt,
Invited cavalry's thunder. No Howard!
His heart leaped. One charge—and the star!

But Fate, the slut, is flirtatious. What
Miles, in hypnotic passion, did not
See was a network of small, brush-grown coulees,
And a great coulee, moatlike, east and west,
Draining down to the Snake, and top growth
At that distance looked like the leveling plain.
This, Miles could not see, but clear to his sight,
If not to his brain, there was, beyond,
A long ridge, now brown with autumn-bit sage to give
Perfect deception for braves to lie in,
Barrel steady, trigger-finger looped, eye squinting.

How calm the plain looked. In saintly peace
Miles stood in God's love. He knew that God loved him.
For at the debouchment of Bear Paws there was
No perspective to show, in the dip, swell and dip,
That the last east-west cross-ridge, southward,
That looked so easy, lied.
The easiest yet, it looked,
For eastward
It sinks. Ah, how in his dream could he know
That on the far side, on the north,
Before the flat of the village, it dropped sharp
To hoof-trap and haunch-grind that, sudden,

Would crumple the cavalry eastward, and spill it,
Tangled and cramped, directly under
The rifle-pricked ridge beyond,
And the closer spite of the fanged coulee?

That is what the land-lay today indicates.

Miles saw in his head the victory form like a crystal—
With Companies *A, D,* and *K* of Custer's
Old favorite Seventh, with Cheyenne scouts,
Who could not now for scouting be used
For fear of alarm,
As the cutting edge of attack.

His breath comes hard. How slow the bastards find place!
Already the Cheyennes, now slick-skinned and naked
To breech-clout and moccasins, hold back
Pawing mounts, though they pant to ride
For the kill, to make *coup,*
To dab cheek with the blood of a brother.
They yelp in the snow-swirl. Captain Hale jokes:
"My God, have I got to go out and get killed
In such weather?" It was a good joke. But no laughter.

No Howard yet! Miles lifts his arm.
He takes the deep breath. He shouts, "Attack!"

He thought of the half-wits down there, scarce more
Than a hundred. *What were they thinking down there?*

There was only silence down there.

*

Now is the rhythm of hoof. First, trot:
Down slope, down dip, up ridge-swell,
Then down. Then bursts the hoof-thunder!—
And then the blind surge when the last
Ridge divulges its dire,
Deadly secret, compresses the ranks, swerves horsemen, and spills
The mass to the open before the moat-coulee. Blaze
Now has burst, bursts first
At two hundred, a hundred and fifty, a hundred, then fifty
Long paces, but not long for lead, and the charge,
Like sea-froth at cliff-foot, in blood-spume
Shatters:

Horses rearing in death, the death scream, saddles
Blown empty, lines broken, all officers down, pure panic.
Now Death probes out for the backbone, for shoulders,
At Enfield—at Winchester—at Sharps range,
Snow red, then redder,
And reddening more, as snow falls
From the unperturbed gray purity of sky.

Captain Hale was a prophet: dead in such weather.

> *I never went up against anything like the Nez Perces in all*
> *my life, and I have been in a lot of scraps.*
>
> JAMES SNELL, SCOUT FOR MILES

Miles's infantry made out some better; took losses, of course,
But in dying laid down a ring of investment, which promised a siege.

So the siege settled down,
With slow, systematic shelling of all in the village,
And hunger began its long gut-gnaw.

For Miles, what bastardly luck! A siege—and how long?

But luck held for Miles. Under the fire
Of cannon buried howitzerwise, what else
But negotiation? It came—with Miles
Violating a flag of truce to hold Joseph.
But the braves were alert. They, too, grabbed a hostage.
So terms were arranged, Miles's terms mysteriously generous.

Now Howard stands, suddenly, there.

Stood there, commander, enduring the only
Outlet of rage and hatred Miles
Could give vent to: ironical courtesy, cold,
Gray as snot. But Howard,
Whose sweat had soaked sheets in wrestling with God,
Laid his remaining hand on the steel-stiff shoulder
That quivered beneath it. Howard, almost
As soft as a whisper, promises him the surrender.

And hearing his own words, he knew a pure
And never-before-known bliss swell his heart.

Miles laughed with the laughter of friend or brother.
But if Howard smiled, the smile was inward—
A fact unnoticed by Miles, who already

Was deep in his head's dizzy darkness composing
The rhetoric of his official communiqué:

> *We have had our usual success. We made a very direct and*
> *rapid march across country, and after a severe engagement*
> *and being kept under fire for three days, the hostile camp*
> *under Chief Joseph surrendered at two o'clock today.*

How now would the newspapers blaze! Sherman smile!
And let old Sturgis—a colonel yet—bite his nails.
To hell with his son—all soldiers die.

> *I felt the end coming. All for which we had suffered and*
> *lost! Thoughts came of Wallowa, where I grew up . . .*
> *Then with a rifle I stand forth, saying in my heart, 'Here I*
> *will die.'*
>
> YELLOW WOLF

But did not. Lived on. In history.

Five inches of snow now, sky gray, and yonder
One buffalo rug, black on white,
And kept white until Howard, Miles, and the staff
Would arrive when the hour struck.
It would strike.

For terms now are firm: rifles stacked
With bandoliers twined. No need now for rifles,
For hunting or honor. They'd go to Keogh

And eat white man's bread, with only the promise
Of Miles that in spring they'd go west to high land
Where mountains are snow-white and the Great Spirit
Spills peace into the heart of man.
Wallowa—no! But another land of pure air,
Blue distance, white peaks, their own lives to live,
And again their own guns, to hunt as man must.
And there they might think of the eyes of the fathers
Yet on them, though across all
The mountains, the distance, the noble disaster.

> *I believed General Miles or I never would have surrendered.*
>
> CHIEF JOSEPH

At late afternoon, light failing, Howard
Is called, with his brass, to the buffalo robe that
Lies black against snow. Up from the dry
Brown gravel and water-round stones of the Eagle,
Now going snow-white in dryness, and up
From the shell-churned
Chaos of camp-site, slowly ascends
The procession. Joseph, not straight, sits his mount,
Head forward bowed, scalp lock with otter-skin tied.

Black braids now framed a face past pain.
Hands loose before him, the death-giving rifle
Loose-held across, he comes first.
The bullet scar is on his brow.
Chief Hush-hush-kute, beside him, on foot,
Moves, and that chief speaks, and the head

Of Joseph is bowed, bowed as in courtesy
To words of courage and comfort. But
The head may be bowed to words by others unheard.

Joseph draws in his mount. Then,
As though all years were naught in their count, arrow-straight
He suddenly sits, head now lifted. With perfect ease
To the right he swings a buckskinned leg over. Stands.
His gray shawl exhibits four bullet holes.

Straight standing, he thrusts out his rifle,
Muzzle-grounded, to Howard. It is
The gesture, straight-flung, of one who casts the world away.

Howard smiles as a friend. But
Peremptory or contemptuous,
Indicates Miles. Upon that steel symbol,
The hand of Miles closes. We do not know
What ambiguities throttle his heart.
Miles is sunk in his complex tension of being,
In his moment of triumph and nakedness.

Joseph steps back. His heart gives words.
But the words, translated, are addressed to Howard.

> *Tell General Howard I know his heart. What he told me*
> *before I have in my heart. I am tired of fighting. Our chiefs*
> *are killed. Looking Glass is dead. The old men are killed. It*
> *is the young men who say yes or no. He (*) who led the*

(*) Ollokot, brother of Joseph

young men is dead. It is cold and we have no blankets. Our
little children are freezing to death. I want time to look for
my children and see how many of them I may find. Maybe
I shall find them among the dead. Hear me, my chiefs, I am
tired. Heart is sick and sad. From where the sun now
stands, I will fight no more forever.

Then Joseph drew his blanket over his head.

VII

At Keogh they ate the white man's bread.
The taste was gray to a prisoner's tongue.
Then Bismarck, then Leavenworth, far off in Kansas,
On one side a river. Before ice came, edges
Were streaked, slick, slow. It crawled.
But when sun in its season came back, its wrath
Might suck up green bubbles of slime, to burst.
On the other side a fat lagoon lolled
With dead fish floating, belly-white upward,
And all water foul for cooking or drinking.
As early heat grew, by daylight or night,
Night moonlit or dark, insects unremitting
Were whirring or sizzling like lust in the blood;
Or the sound the lust of murder makes
In the deep of your heart before the stroke.

Ah, when would the terms of the promise be kept!
When would the word of Miles set them
Among promised mountains, far blueness, far whiteness?
How could they know that Miles, whom they trusted,
Was only a brigadier behind whom
Moved forces, faceless, timeless, dim,
And in such dimness, merciless?

Did Joseph now ever think, and with
What twisted irony, of the name—
If he knew it—of that man who
Held life and death in his hands, and who
Had broken the terms of surrender, and sent
Them to Leavenworth to die?
General Sherman, it was, and the name he bore,
That of the greatest Indian chief—
Tecumseh. William Tecumseh Sherman, of course.

Perhaps Joseph prayed, but could not die.
And living, lived for one thing only—to see
The terms of surrender maintained, and his people
Again in their high land,
Where men love earth and earth loves man,
And men eat food that earth, in love, gives.

*

With agents, with bosses, Joseph spoke,
With inspectors, with officers, getting no heed.
Only one man, with an uneasy conscience, might
Speak out the truth, and the truth be heard,
And was it integrity, or some
Sad division of self, torn in ambition
And ambition's price, that at last made Miles
The only staunch friend of Joseph for all
The years? In his rising success, did something make Miles
Wonder what was the price of a star?

And was it the friendship of Miles that got Joseph to Hayes
To fill the presidential ear with his old story?
Using Yellow Bull to speak, he spoke
To the Great White Father, but old Hayes
Knew his profession, so Joseph was sent to sit
With busy commissioners to say,
"It makes my heart turn sick when I
Remember all the good, kind words
And broken promises." He told
The bounty white men had sometimes paid
For a red scalp—the going rate,
One hundred dollars per buck, fifty
Per woman, only twenty-five for a child's.

*A party of miners returned to Owyhee from a raid on
Indians with twenty scalps and some plunder. The miners
are well.*

THE PORTLAND <u>OREGONIAN</u>

In the *North American Review,* Joseph's words,
Translated, were published—
The fraud of, the suffering of, his people, the lies,
The thoughts of his heart. Thousands, bored, read.
Some read, remembered. Felt their hearts stir.

VIII

It took all the years. To the Northwest, but not Wallowa,
At last, honed down by the old torment and Time,
The people came. But on a reservation in Washington,
Joseph sits, can stir thence only by permit.

"They built me a house at Nespelem—
After many had died by the stinking river,
Where death rose on the air of evening
And bellies of dead fish float, bloated white,
In moonlight. In that stinking land we left
Our last dead. Did at last they dream of our mountains?
But mothers remember the names left there,
Still sacred in stink, and children
Remember the names that there sleep. The old
Who there sleep, sleep on the sweetest of pillows—the knowledge
Of what it is to be brave in your time. Their eyes
Fix on us as they lie in their darkness.

"They built me a house—me, a chief,
Who had lifted the death-tube, Winchester or Sharps,
And peered at the blue spot the sight leveled to
In nameless election. I slow squeezed trigger.
The blue spot was still.
For me, a chief—as though I were one
Of the white half-men who scratch in the ground

And at evening slop hogs. For me,
Who had lain on the prairie in starlight
And heard the coyote-wail of the far scout.

"No foot of mine ever crossed that doorsill.
I pitched my tepee on earth. I lay there.
At evening I stared at my camp-coals and wondered
If, snared in my error and weakness, I
Had managed at least some pinch of rightness. I prayed
That my father, whose eyes see all, and judge,
Might find some worth in an act of mine,
However slight.

"I sit, coals simmering,
A dying animal humped with no motion under
Darkness of skies that reach out forever
While forever stars spin what patterns
The Great Spirit's heart defines. I—
I only a dot in dimness—think
Of my father and yearn only
That he can think me a man
Worthy the work in dark of his loins.

"But what is a man? An autumn-tossed aspen,
Pony-fart in the wind, the melting of snow-slush?
Yes, that is all. Unless—unless—
We can learn to live the Great Spirit's meaning
As the old and wise grope for it.
And my heart swells when I remember
That day at Snake Creek when Miles surprised us,

And I, herding horses, no gun, ran,
Through bullet-song and scream of the hit ones,
Back to my tepee, but before
I touched, the slot had opened and my own
Wife's hand thrust forth the rifle, and only
One word came: *Fight*. Now all I remember
Is how her eyes gleam in dream-darkness, forever."

At night, coals wink from the heart of years,
But when he rises, the years fall away
Like leaves from a great oak in autumn to show
The indestructible structure.
To a height uncommon to men the head rises
In upward straightness, framed by braids fading,
The face like bronze hardened long back from the mold,
Nose thrusting, the thrust of jawbone, the downward
Decisive will-thrust of lips where they join
On each cheek-side. If you gaze at him,
Eyes you gaze into will seem but to show
The mirror of distance behind you, far,
And the mirror of Time that brings you both here,
And will, in time, part you forever.

Frozen, you stand in that moment of final assessment.

He is famous now. Great men have come
To shake his hand in his poverty.
Generals who chased him, ten to one,
With their fancy equipment, Gatling guns,
Artillery. Histories name him a genius.

And even Sherman, who never had fought him
But gave more death than ever his subordinate generals—
Yes, slime-green waters of Leavenworth—wrote:

> *The Indians throughout displayed a courage and skill that*
> *elicited universal praise; they abstained from scalping; let*
> *captive women go free; and did not commit indiscriminate*
> *murders of peaceful families . . . they fought with almost*
> *scientific skill.*

Frontiersmen, land-grabbers, gold-panners were dead.
Veterans of the long chase skull-grinned in darkness.
A more soft-handed ilk now swayed the West. They founded
Dynasties, universities, libraries, shuffled
Stocks, and occasionally milked
The Treasury of the United States,
Not to mention each other. They slick-fucked a land.

But as their wealth grew, so Joseph's fame.
As the President's guest, in the White House,
He had shaken Roosevelt's hand. With Miles,
No longer a mere brigadier, he broke
Bread among crystal and silver. Back West
Artists came to commemorate for the future
That noble head. In bronze it was cast:

> *In gallery 224 of the American wing of the Metropolitan*
> *Museum of Art, accession number 06.313, may be found*
> *the bronze portrait of*

'Joseph, Chief of the Nez Perce Indians. His Indian name, Hin-mah-toó-yah-lat-kekht, is said to mean Thunder Rolling in the Mountains . . . This medallion was taken from life in 1889. Bronze, diameter 17-1/2 in. Signed Olin L. Warner . . .'

AMERICAN SCULPTURE CATALOGUE

OF THE COLLECTION OF THE METROPOLITAN

MUSEUM OF ART, PAGE 42

Great honor came, for it came to pass
That to praise the red man was the way
Best adapted to expunge all, all, in the mist
Of bloodless myth. And in the predictably obscene
Procession to dedicate Grant's Tomb, which grandeur
Was now to hold the poor, noble dust of Appomattox,
Joseph, whose people had never taken
A scalp, rode beside Buffalo Bill—
Who had once sent his wife a yet-warm scalp,
He himself had sliced from the pate
Of a red man who'd missed him. Joseph rode
Beside Buffalo Bill, who broke clay pigeons—
One-two-three-four-five—just like that.

Joseph rode by the clown, the magician who could transform
For howling patriots, or royalty,
The blood of history into red ketchup,
A favorite American condiment. By his side
Joseph rode. Did Joseph know
Of the bloody scalp in love's envelope, know

That the dead Grant had once, in the White House,
In his own hand, certified the land
Of the Winding Waters to Joseph's people—
"Forever"—until some western politico, or such,
Jerked him by the nose, like a bull with a brass
Ring there for control?

Not right, not left,
Joseph looked, as hoofs on the cobbles clacked
In the dolor of that procession. He
Was only himself, and the distances
He stared into were only himself.

After all the years back at Nespelem,
In Washington, not the Land of the Winding Waters,
No right to move without permission,
He wore the poor dress of his people. The great
War-bonnet, whose eagle feathers had gleamed in
Ceremonial grandeur, grander than life,
Lay locked in a box. Only twice
Permission was given him to go to the Winding Waters.

"The grave of my father lay in a land now tilled
By the white man who owned it, but had something human of heart.
No plowshare had wounded the earth where my father slept,
And the mercy of stones was piled to forbid.
I gazed at the stones. My eyes were dim.
I lifted my eyes that they might be washed
In the purity of the distance of mountains.
I thought of the purity of that poor man's heart."

*

56

Back at Nespelem, by the campfire,
Did Joseph wonder if the gaze of Old Joseph
Yet fixed on him?

At least, no sacred land had he ever sold.

At last, he said: "I shall see
But one more snow." Face painted, the body,
Adorned for its rank, awaited the shaman
To rise and speak, and lay the tall ghost.
The earthly possessions among friends were scattered.

But this not the end:
Next year at the second death-feast, Yellow Bull,
Now forking the dead hero's war-horse, rehearses
The tale and its greatness. The coffin
Is opened, and that face for the last time seen
By the Real People. But only by them. It is shut,
And thrust beneath the expensive monument
Of white generosity—that seizes all in the end.

More than twenty years passed before the Nimipu
Dug up what was left
Of Old Joseph still in the cornfield, and took it
To a shore of the Winding Waters, and there
Set up, in sight of snowy peaks, their stone. It was theirs.

This was all that remained them,
After Little Bear Paws and Snake Creek's bitter waters.

IX

To Snake Creek, a century later, I came.

La Guardia to O'Hare, American Airlines, October 9, 1981,
Ticket 704 982 1454 4, Chicago. By Northwest to Great
Falls. Met by two friends, Stuart Wright and David
Quammen.

Out of Great Falls, north, in the Honda,
Out on the swell of infinite plains,
By wash or coulee here and there slashed,
Vacant of cattle, horse, man, the color
Gray-brown, the season October, not yet
Snowfall. Low ramparts of cloud, dark blue,
Hug the horizon westward like
A mountain range shrunken in distance,
But solid, supporting the arch of the sky.
Correspondingly eastward, the dark blue rampart
Is topped by a lacing of pale, pale gold,
Where sun lies in wait.

Springs forth, and distance
In all directions flees, devouring
The scraggle of villages dropped by history on
Route 87. Far off, a gold clump

Of cottonwood shows ranchstead or waterhole.
Sky shudders from blue to the apex of near-white. Onward,

We plunge, northeast, but in our minds see
Only one small black dot,
Which is the Honda creeping slow
Across a large map outspread. Next morning,
At a map-point called Chinook, southward we turn.
Tires now grind gravel. Right, west,
Plains swell to the sweep of arrogant skyline.
Now southwest, the skyline begins to rise, to heave, to crumple,
To darken. There, at last, are
The Little Bear Paw Mountains, lifting
In curves dulled by ages, but some, a few yet,
Snag angrily skyward, snow-smeared. Then eastward
They swing, suck the plain up in blueness. This
Is the hump that had once hidden Miles.

We turn left at the sign. There
Are the modest monuments. First,
A bronze plate, in stone set, and
In relief, a soldier (presumably Miles), and before him
An Indian, tall, half-naked, one arm lifted skyward,
And beneath, the words of Joseph:
"From where the sun now stands, I will fight
No more forever."

There is the map,
Large, enamel on metal, weatherproof:
Analysis of the action. And then,

The large bronze plate on granite propped
By the Republic to honor the name
Of every trooper who, in glory, had died here.

But the troopers who died here, who obediently died
For the ego of Miles, did not rot here. That final
Process was achieved with those who in Custer's
Dream died, when, at the Little Big Horn,
He at last had salted the tail of
That idiot phantasm of immortality.

The map shows here a mass grave
Where, no doubt, red flesh had rotted.
But not all the red flesh, for when the siege-line
Had tightened, and shells began lobbing in,
The Indians tried to dig caves for children,
The women, the old. So shells spared
Later some spade-work for blue-bellies.

You see the heaved earth, now mollified.

Snake Creek loops away, is hidden in thickets
Of last leaves of wild rose, now dusty crimson of leaf,
Branches studded with red hips. You tear through briars
Shoulder-high. Snake Creek is near-dry, only
A string of mossy-green puddles where Joseph,
In the same season,
Had once found water fresh for people and horse herd.

Beyond is the raised alluvial flat

Where tepees stood. There, southward, a steel pipe,
With marker screwed on, defines the spot
Of the tepee of Joseph.

If you climb the slope, say a mile and a half,
Or two, to the point where Miles must first
Have debouched from the Bear Paws, and look north,
You see what he saw—or what erosion has done.
Did he send his Cheyennes
To scout the lay, or did his star dance
In its passionate certainty? No,
Not the Cheyennes—to ruin surprise.
Northward, you see what you guess he saw
In his manic snatch for glory—the village,
The downward plain-sweep, swell and dip, swell and dip,
Cunt-open and panting, inviting the picture-book cavalry stroke.

Now, as you wander brown sage, you find
Steel pipes thrust in where each man died—
If he was white or of consequence.
There are markers screwed on with a name: *Poker Joe,*
Who knew the guile of the Yellowstone,
Ollokot, brother and warrior peerless,
And *Looking Glass,* war-chief, the cunning in council.
And names of the troopers, including the jokester
Captain Hale, who died in such weather.
And you find the spot marked where the buffalo robe
Once lay black on snow, and Howard, with what
Compassion or irony, gestured to Miles.

*

Alone on that last spot I stood, my friends
Now prowling and far on the high land. No snow
Now on brown grass or red leaf
Or black buffalo robe ceremonially swept
To its blackness. All
Now only a picture there in my head—

And there
He stands, the gray shawl showing
The four bullet holes, and hoofprints seen
In now hypothetical snow,
Marking the way he had come. I,
In fanatic imagination, saw—
No, see—the old weapon
Outthrust, firm in a hand that does not
Tremble. I see lips move, but
No sound hear.

I see him who in how many midnights
Had stood—what seasons?—while the susurrus
Of tribal sleep dies toward what stars,
While he, eyes fixed on what strange stars, knew
That eyes were fixed on him, eyes of
Those fathers that incessantly, with
The accuracy of that old Winchester, rifled
Through all, through darkness, distance, Time,
To know if he had proved a man, and being
A man, would make all those
Who now there slept know
Their own manhood.

*

He knew—could see afar, beyond all night—
Those ancient eyes, in which love and judgment
Hold equal glitter, and, with no blink,
Strove always toward him. And he—
He strove to think of things outside
Of Time, in some
Great whirling sphere, like truth unnamable. Thus—
Standing there, he might well,
Already in such midnight, have foreknown
The end.

But could not know that, after
The end, his own manhood, burnished
Only in the glow of his endless pity, would shine.

I saw
Vastness of plains lifting in twilight for
Winter's cold kiss, its absoluteness. Thought
Of the squirming myriads far at
My back. Then thought of the mayor
Of Spokane—whoever the hell he may have been.

But suddenly knew that for those sound
Of heart there is no ultimate
Irony. There is only
Process, which is one name for history. Often
Pitiful. But, sometimes, under
The scrutinizing prism of Time,
Triumphant.

*

I heard shouts of friends, closer.
Now soon they would go back, I too,
Into the squirming throng, faceless to facelessness,
And under a lower sky. But wondered,
Even so, if when the traffic light
Rings green, some stranger may pause and thus miss
His own mob's rush to go where the light
Says go, and pausing, may look,
Not into a deepening shade of canyon,
Nor, head now up, toward ice peak in moonlight white,
But, standing paralyzed in his momentary eternity, into
His own heart look while he asks
From what undefinable distance, years, and direction,
Eyes of fathers are suddenly fixed on him. To know.

I turned to my friend Quammen, the nearer. Called:
"It's getting night, and a hell of a way
To go." We went,
And did not talk much on the way.

ROBERT PENN WARREN was born in Guthrie, Kentucky, in 1905. After graduating summa cum laude from Vanderbilt University (1925), he received a master's degree from the University of California (1927), and did graduate work at Yale University (1927–28) and at Oxford as a Rhodes Scholar (B. Litt., 1930).

Mr. Warren has published many books, including ten novels, fifteen volumes of poetry, and a volume of short stories; also a play, a collection of critical essays, a biography, three historical essays, a critical book on Dreiser and a study of Melville, and two studies of race relations in America. This body of work has been published in a period of fifty-two years—a period during which Mr. Warren has also had an active career as a professor of English.

All the King's Men (1946) was awarded the Pulitzer Prize for Fiction. The Shelley Memorial Award recognized Mr. Warren's early poems. *Promises* (1957) won the Pulitzer Prize for Poetry, the Edna St. Vincent Millay Prize for the Poetry Society of America, and the National Book Award. In 1944–45 Mr. Warren was the second occupant of the Chair of Poetry at the Library of Congress. In 1952 he was elected to the American Philosophical Society; in 1959 to the American Academy of Arts and Letters; and in 1975 to the American Academy of Arts and Sciences. In 1967 he received the Bollingen Prize in Poetry for *Selected Poems: New and Old, 1923–1966*, and in 1970 the National Medal for Literature, and the Van Wyck Brooks Award for the book-length poem *Audubon: A Vision*. In 1974 he was chosen by the National Endowment for the Humanities to deliver the third Annual Jefferson Lecture in the Humanities. In 1975 he received the Emerson-Thoreau Award of the American Academy of Arts and Sciences. In 1976 he received the Copernicus Award from the Academy of American Poets, in recognition of his career but with special notice of *Or Else—Poem/Poems 1968–1974*. In 1977 he received the Harriet Monroe Prize for Poetry and the Wilma and Roswell Messing, Jr. Award. In 1979, for *Now and Then*, a book of new poems, he received his third Pulitzer

Prize. In 1980 he received the Award of the Connecticut Arts Council, the Presidential Medal of Freedom, the Common Wealth Award for Literature, and the Hubbell Memorial Award (The Modern Language Association). In 1981 he was a recipient of a Prize Fellowship of the John D. and Catherine T. MacArthur Foundation.

Mr. Warren lives in Connecticut with his wife, Eleanor Clark (author of *The Bitter Box, Rome and a Villa, The Oysters of Locmariaquer, Baldur's Gate, Eyes, Etc.: A Memoir,* and *Gloria Mundi*). They have two children, Rosanna and Gabriel.